Shadow Work Journal Prompts

By M.m.Adina

M.m.Adina 2024

The "Shadow Work Journal Prompts" book serves as a comprehensive tool for individuals seeking to embark on a transformative journey of self-reflection and growth.

A Brief Biography

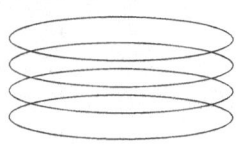 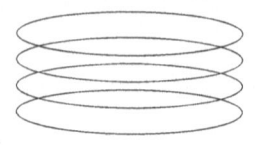

Book Description:

IIn Shadow Work Journal Prompts by M. M. Adina, takes readers on a profound journey of self-discovery and transformation. Drawing on her background in transpersonal psychology and a approaches, Adina invites readers to explore the uncharted territories of their inner selves.

This transformative journal is more than a collection of writing exercises; it's a companion on the journey toward self-acceptance, empowerment, and a deeper understanding of one's authentic nature.

Dive into the depths of self-discovery with "Shadow Work Journal Prompts." Crafted by an insightful guide, these prompts serve as a compass for your journey through the unexplored territories of your psyche. Explore suppressed emotions, confront fears, and unravel hidden patterns as you navigate a transformative path towards self-acceptance. This journal is more than pages—it's an intimate companion, offering profound insights and guiding you toward a richer understanding of your authentic self. Embrace the shadows, illuminate your inner landscape, and embark on a voyage of personal growth with each thoughtfully curated prompt.

BELONGS TO :

_____

_____

_____

# Introduction:

1. Exploring the Shadows:
- What emotions or traits do you typically avoid or suppress in yourself?
- Can you identify a recurring pattern or theme in challenging situations you've faced? What might it reveal about your shadow self?

2. Facing Fears:
- What fears or anxieties hold you back from pursuing your goals or dreams?
- Reflect on a past failure. What lessons can you extract from that experience, and how might it be linked to your deeper fears?

3. Unmasking Beliefs:
- What limiting beliefs about yourself do you carry? Where did they originate, and how do they affect your choices?
- Explore an area of your life where you feel stuck. What beliefs might be contributing to this stagnation?

4. Embracing Imperfections:
- List three qualities or aspects of yourself that you've labeled as "imperfect." How might these be valuable or contribute to your uniqueness?
- Reflect on a mistake you've made. How can you reframe it as an opportunity for growth rather than a failure?

5. Relationship Dynamics:
- Identify patterns in your relationships. Do you notice recurring themes or conflicts? How might these patterns be connected to your shadow aspects?
- Consider a person who triggers strong emotions in you. What might their behavior be reflecting about your own unresolved issues?

Introduction:

5. Relationship Dynamics:

- Identify patterns in your relationships. Do you notice recurring themes or conflicts? How might these patterns be connected to your shadow aspects?
- Consider a person who triggers strong emotions in you. What might their behavior be reflecting about your own unresolved issues?

6. Forgiveness and Compassion:

- Reflect on a past hurt or betrayal. Can you find it in yourself to forgive and release the associated pain?
- Explore a situation where you've judged others harshly. What does this judgment reveal about your own insecurities or unacknowledged traits?

7. Reconnecting with Joy:

- Recall a childhood activity that brought you pure joy. How can you reintegrate elements of that joy into your adult life?
- Identify activities or hobbies you've neglected. How might embracing these passions contribute to a more fulfilled and balanced life?

8. Balancing Masculine and Feminine Energies:

- Consider the balance of masculine and feminine energies within yourself. Do you notice an imbalance, and how does it impact your decision-making and relationships?
- Reflect on societal expectations regarding gender roles. How have these expectations influenced your self-perception?

Consider the balance of masculine and feminine energies within yourself.

Do you notice an imbalance, and how does it impact your decision-making and relationships?

Reflect on societal expectations regarding gender roles.

How have these expectations influenced your self-perception?

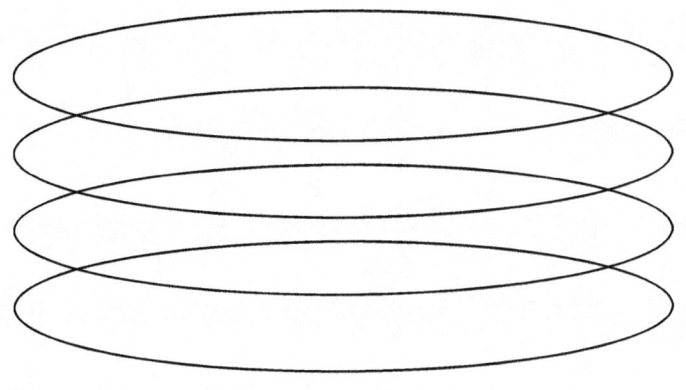

date:

| MON | TUE | WED | THU | FRI | SAT | SUN |

1. What is a fear that you've never shared with anyone?

PROMPTS

date:

| MON | TUE | WED | THU | FRI | SAT | SUN |

2. Describe a time when you felt deeply ashamed of yourself.

date:

| MON | TUE | WED | THU | FRI | SAT | SUN |

3. Write about a recurring dream or nightmare and its significance.

date:

| MON | TUE | WED | THU | FRI | SAT | SUN |

4. Explore a childhood memory that still haunts you.

date:

| MON | TUE | WED | THU | FRI | SAT | SUN |

5. List the traits or behaviors in others that trigger you. Why do they trigger you?

date:

| MON | TUE | WED | THU | FRI | SAT | SUN |

6. Write a letter to your younger self offering support and guidance.

date:

| MON | TUE | WED | THU | FRI | SAT | SUN |

7. What is the biggest lie you've ever told, and why did you tell it?

date:

| MON | TUE | WED | THU | FRI | SAT | SUN |

8. Describe a situation where you felt powerless and explore the emotions that arose.

date:

| MON | TUE | WED | THU | FRI | SAT | SUN |

9. What are your most self-destructive habits, and what triggers them?

date:

| MON | TUE | WED | THU | FRI | SAT | SUN |

10. Write about a time when you felt overwhelmed by jealousy.

date:

| MON | TUE | WED | THU | FRI | SAT | SUN |

11. Explore the earliest memory you have of feeling rejected.

date:

| MON | TUE | WED | THU | FRI | SAT | SUN |

12. Describe a relationship that ended badly and what you learned from it

date:

| MON | TUE | WED | THU | FRI | SAT | SUN |

13. Explore your most significant regret and what you could learn from it

date:

| MON | TUE | WED | THU | FRI | SAT | SUN |

14. What are your most critical inner voices or self-doubts, and where do they come from?

date:

| MON | TUE | WED | THU | FRI | SAT | SUN |

15. Explore your feelings about your body and appearance.

date:

| MON | TUE | WED | THU | FRI | SAT | SUN |

16. Write about a time you felt abandoned or neglected.

date:

| MON | TUE | WED | THU | FRI | SAT | SUN |

17. Reflect on a secret you've never shared and why it remains hidden

18. Describe an experience of loss or grief and its impact on your life

date:

| MON | TUE | WED | THU | FRI | SAT | SUN |

19. Write about your relationship with your parents, both positive and negative aspects.

date:

| MON | TUE | WED | THU | FRI | SAT | SUN |

20. Reflect on a time when you held a grudge against someone and how it affected you.

| MON | TUE | WED | THU | FRI | SAT | SUN |

21. Describe a situation when you were a bystander to injustice and why you didn't act.

date:

| MON | TUE | WED | THU | FRI | SAT | SUN |

22. Write about a time when you judged someone unfairly and what you learned.

date:

| MON | TUE | WED | THU | FRI | SAT | SUN |

23. Reflect on your biggest insecurities and their origins.

date:

| MON | TUE | WED | THU | FRI | SAT | SUN |

24. Describe a situation when you ignored your intuition and regretted it.

date:

| MON | TUE | WED | THU | FRI | SAT | SUN |

25. Explore your relationship with sexuality and past experiences.

date:

| MON | TUE | WED | THU | FRI | SAT | SUN |

26. Reflect on your relationship with authority figures.

date:

| MON | TUE | WED | THU | FRI | SAT | SUN |

27. . Describe a situation when you silenced your own desires.

date:

| MON | TUE | WED | THU | FRI | SAT | SUN |

28. Write about a time when you felt like an imposter in your career.

date:

| MON | TUE | WED | THU | FRI | SAT | SUN |

29. Reflect on a time when you sabotaged your own success.

date:

| MON | TUE | WED | THU | FRI | SAT | SUN |

30. Write about a situation when you felt like you were not taken seriously

date:

| MON | TUE | WED | THU | FRI | SAT | SUN |

31. Reflect on a time when you felt like an outsider in your own family.

date:

| MON | TUE | WED | THU | FRI | SAT | SUN |

32. Write about a situation where you were overly controlling or manipulative.

date:

| MON | TUE | WED | THU | FRI | SAT | SUN |

33. Write about a time when you felt like you were carrying the weight of the past

| MON | TUE | WED | THU | FRI | SAT | SUN |

34. Write about a situation when you were too focused on other people's opinions.

| MON | TUE | WED | THU | FRI | SAT | SUN |

date:

35. Write about a time when you neglected your creative or artistic side

PROMPTS date:

| MON | TUE | WED | THU | FRI | SAT | SUN |

36. Explore your relationship with spirituality and the divine, or lack thereof.

PROMPTS date:

| MON | TUE | WED | THU | FRI | SAT | SUN |

37. Reflect on a time when you felt like you were living a double life.

date:

| MON | TUE | WED | THU | FRI | SAT | SUN |

38. Write about a time when you pushed people away to protect yourself.

date:

| MON | TUE | WED | THU | FRI | SAT | SUN |

39. Describe a situation when you experienced a significant failure.

date:

| MON | TUE | WED | THU | FRI | SAT | SUN |

40. Explore your beliefs about happiness and your own pursuit of it.

date:

| MON | TUE | WED | THU | FRI | SAT | SUN |

41. Reflect on a time when you felt like you were not in control of your life.

date:

| MON | TUE | WED | THU | FRI | SAT | SUN |

42. Write about a time when you chose to be ignorant about something important.

date:

| MON | TUE | WED | THU | FRI | SAT | SUN |

43. Explore your relationship with self-criticism and self-compassion.

date:

| MON | TUE | WED | THU | FRI | SAT | SUN |

44. Reflect on a time when you engaged in self-sabotage in your career.

date:

| MON | TUE | WED | THU | FRI | SAT | SUN |

45. Write about a situation when you avoided facing a difficult truth.

date:

| MON | TUE | WED | THU | FRI | SAT | SUN |

46. Describe a time when you felt like you were carrying the weight of the world on your shoulders.

date:

| MON | TUE | WED | THU | FRI | SAT | SUN |

47. Explore your beliefs about love and what you believe you deserve.

date:

| MON | TUE | WED | THU | FRI | SAT | SUN |

48. Reflect on a time when you tried to be invisible to avoid conflict.

date:

| MON | TUE | WED | THU | FRI | SAT | SUN |

49. Write about a time when you felt like you were stuck in the past.

| MON | TUE | WED | THU | FRI | SAT | SUN |

date:

49. Write about a time when you felt like you were stuck in the past.

date:

| MON | TUE | WED | THU | FRI | SAT | SUN |

50. Describe a situation when you put others' needs before your own.

51. Reflect on a time when you felt like you were overshadowed by someone else.

52. Write about a situation when you felt like you were playing a role.

MON	TUE	WED	THU	FRI	SAT	SUN

53. Write about a time when you used humor to mask your pain.

date:

| MON | TUE | WED | THU | FRI | SAT | SUN |

54. Reflect on a time when you neglected your mental health.

| MON | TUE | WED | THU | FRI | SAT | SUN |

date:

55. Write about a time when you felt like you were constantly seeking validation

date:

| MON | TUE | WED | THU | FRI | SAT | SUN |

56. Reflect on a time when you were overly self-critical about your achievements.

date:

| MON | TUE | WED | THU | FRI | SAT | SUN |

57. Explore your beliefs about your own potential and what you're capable of.

date:

| MON | TUE | WED | THU | FRI | SAT | SUN |

58. Write about a time when you ignored your own intuition and made a mistake.

date:

| MON | TUE | WED | THU | FRI | SAT | SUN |

59. Explore your relationship with competitiveness and the fear of losing

date:

| MON | TUE | WED | THU | FRI | SAT | SUN |

60. Reflect on a situation when you tried to fix or change someone else.

date:

| MON | TUE | WED | THU | FRI | SAT | SUN |

61. Describe a time when you felt like you were running away from something.

date:

| MON | TUE | WED | THU | FRI | SAT | SUN |

62. Describe a time when you felt like you were sabotaging your own happiness.

63. Explore your relationship with self-sufficiency and asking for help.

date:

| MON | TUE | WED | THU | FRI | SAT | SUN |

64. Write about a time when you felt like you were running away from your responsibilities.

| MON | TUE | WED | THU | FRI | SAT | SUN |

65. Write about a time when you felt like you were repeating the same mistakes.

66. Explore your relationship with societal expectations around gender and its impact on your self-identity.

date:

| MON | TUE | WED | THU | FRI | SAT | SUN |

67. Describe a time when you felt like you were hiding your true self from your children.

date:

| MON | TUE | WED | THU | FRI | SAT | SUN |

68. Describe a time when you felt like you were hiding your true self from your children.

date:

| MON | TUE | WED | THU | FRI | SAT | SUN |

69. Reflect on a time when you felt like you were living in the shadows of others

date:

| MON | TUE | WED | THU | FRI | SAT | SUN |

70. Write about a situation when you were overly dependent on someone else.

date:

| MON | TUE | WED | THU | FRI | SAT | SUN |

71. Describe a time when you felt like you were compromising your values for convenience.

date:

| MON | TUE | WED | THU | FRI | SAT | SUN |

72. Explore your beliefs about the role of intuition in your decision-making.

date:

| MON | TUE | WED | THU | FRI | SAT | SUN |

73. Write about a time when you were too focused on past mistakes and regrets.

date:

| MON | TUE | WED | THU | FRI | SAT | SUN |

74. Reflect on a time when you felt like you were carrying the weight of your ancestors' burdens.

| MON | TUE | WED | THU | FRI | SAT | SUN |

75. Describe a situation when you neglected your own emotional healing.

date:

| MON | TUE | WED | THU | FRI | SAT | SUN |

76. Explore your relationship with your inner child and the nurturing it needs.

date:

| MON | TUE | WED | THU | FRI | SAT | SUN |

77. Reflect on a time when you felt like you were stuck in a never-ending cycle.

date:

| MON | TUE | WED | THU | FRI | SAT | SUN |

78. Write about a time when you denied your own desires to maintain the status quo.

date:

| MON | TUE | WED | THU | FRI | SAT | SUN |

79. Describe a time when you felt like you were living a life of constant distraction.

date:

| MON | TUE | WED | THU | FRI | SAT | SUN |

80. Explore your beliefs about the significance of your dreams and aspirations.

| MON | TUE | WED | THU | FRI | SAT | SUN |

81. Reflect on a time when you were too critical of your own spiritual journey.

date:

| MON | TUE | WED | THU | FRI | SAT | SUN |

82. Write about a situation when you felt like you were hiding your true self from the world.

83. Describe a time when you felt like you were trapped by societal expectations.

date:

| MON | TUE | WED | THU | FRI | SAT | SUN |

84. Explore your relationship with your cultural heritage and how it shapes your identity.

date:

| MON | TUE | WED | THU | FRI | SAT | SUN |

85. Reflect on a time when you felt like you were overshadowed by your siblings.

date:

| MON | TUE | WED | THU | FRI | SAT | SUN |

86. Write about a time when you were too judgmental of someone else's choices.

date:

| MON | TUE | WED | THU | FRI | SAT | SUN |

87. Describe a situation when you denied your own wisdom and intuition.

date:

| MON | TUE | WED | THU | FRI | SAT | SUN |

88. Explore your beliefs about societal judgments and how they impact your self-image.

date:

| MON | TUE | WED | THU | FRI | SAT | SUN |

89. Reflect on a time when you felt like you were living a life of pretense.

date:

| MON | TUE | WED | THU | FRI | SAT | SUN |

90. Write about a time when you were too critical of your own body and appearance.

date:

MON	TUE	WED	THU	FRI	SAT	SUN

91. Describe a time when you felt like you were constantly seeking approval from your partner.

| MON | TUE | WED | THU | FRI | SAT | SUN |

92. Explore your relationship with societal ideals of romantic love and its influence.

date:

| MON | TUE | WED | THU | FRI | SAT | SUN |

93. Write about a situation when you were overly attached to your career or job.

date:

| MON | TUE | WED | THU | FRI | SAT | SUN |

94. Reflect on a time when you felt like you were neglecting your physical health.

date:

| MON | TUE | WED | THU | FRI | SAT | SUN |

95. Describe a time when you were too hesitant to pursue your true passions.

date:

| MON | TUE | WED | THU | FRI | SAT | SUN |

96. Explore your beliefs about the role of ambition in your life.

date:

| MON | TUE | WED | THU | FRI | SAT | SUN |

97. Write about a time when you felt like you were sacrificing your well-being for external success.

date:

| MON | TUE | WED | THU | FRI | SAT | SUN |

98. Reflect on a situation when you were overly self-critical about your parenting skills.

99. Describe a time when you felt like you were hiding your true self from your children.

date:

| MON | TUE | WED | THU | FRI | SAT | SUN |

100. Write about a time when you felt like you were competing with someone in your life.

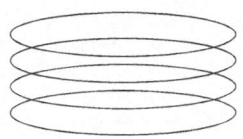

Notes

Subject :

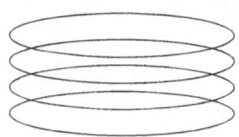

Notes

Subject :

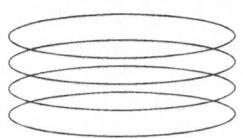

Notes

Subject :

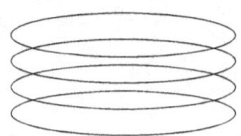

Notes

Subject :

www.ingramcontent.com/pod-product-compliance
Lightning Source LLC
Chambersburg PA
CBHW071008080526
44587CB00015B/2386